# Lobsters

### Kris Hirschmann

**KIDHAVEN PRESS**

*An imprint of Thomson Gale, a part of The Thomson Corporation*

THOMSON

GALE

Detroit • New York • San Francisco • San Diego
New Haven, Conn. • Waterville, Maine • London • Munich

27~

*For more information, contact*
The Gale Group, Inc.
27500 Drake Rd.
Farmington Hills, MI 48331-3535
Or you can visit our Internet site at http://www.gale.com

| LIBRARY OF CONGRESS CATALOGING-IN-PUBLICATION DATA |
| --- |
| Hirschmann, Kris, 1967– |
|    Lobsters / by Kris Hirschmann. |
|      p. cm. — (Creatures of the sea) |
| Summary: Discusses lobster habitat, anatomy, life cycle, hunting methods, and predators. |
|    Includes bibliographical references (p.    ). |
|    ISBN 0-7377-2343-2 (hardback : alk. paper) |
| 1. Lobsters—Juvenile literature. I. title. |
|    QL444.M33H562   2005 |
|    595.3'84—dc22 |
|                                           2004007518 |

Printed in the United States of America

# Table of contents

# Introduction

# Lobster Conservation

In some parts of the world, lobster hunting is big business. America's New England region, especially Maine, is a hot spot of commercial lobstering. Some parts of Australia and northern Europe also support thriving lobster industries. In these areas, hundreds of fishing boats haul millions of lobsters out of the oceans each year. These are then sold to restaurants and grocery stores throughout the world.

Many scientists worry that commercial fisheries are damaging local lobster populations. They fear that if too many lobsters are removed from the sea, not enough will be left to create new generations. As a result, the number of lobsters in certain areas may decline. Local governments are already trying to fix this problem by setting size limits for lobster

*A fisherman shows off one of the millions of lobsters caught each year to be sold in restaurants and grocery stores.*

catches. In other words, if lobsters are not a certain minimum length, the law requires fishermen to throw them back into the ocean. This prevents young lobsters from being taken before they have a chance to grow older and reproduce.

Some people feel that the current size limits are too low. They think lobsters should be allowed to grow older and bigger before they can be caught. Other people think the current limits are fine. Fishermen also point out that they regulate themselves by throwing "eggers" (egg-bearing females) back into the water, even if the females are above the legal size limit. The fishermen cut notches in the tails of these lobsters before they release them. If a notched female is caught again, she will be released even if she is not carrying eggs. Fishermen know that proven egg layers must survive if lobster populations are to remain healthy.

At present, lobsters are plentiful throughout the world's oceans. Even if populations get smaller in certain areas, these animals will be in no danger of overall extinction. This is fortunate since the oceans would be much less interesting if these amazing animals were ever to disappear.

# Lobster Bodies and Basics

Lobsters belong to a group of animals called the **crustaceans**. Lobsters account for only about 150 of the roughly 26,000 crustacean species. This is a very small percentage. What lobsters lack in numbers, however, they make up in size. These animals are giants in the crustacean family, which contains many tiny creatures. Because lobsters are so big compared to their relatives, they are among the world's best-recognized crustaceans.

Lobster species are divided into four groups: true lobsters, spiny lobsters, slipper or shovel lobsters, and deep-sea lobsters. The common lobsters of North America and northern Europe, which are part of the true lobster group, are especially well known and well studied. Scientists also know a lot about the very common spiny lobsters.

## Where Lobsters Are Found

All lobsters are saltwater creatures and all species are bottom dwellers. Lobsters seem to prefer rocky bottoms or coral reefs because they have lots of holes and cracks for shelter. Lobsters may also dig burrows in muddy bottoms if they cannot find a rocky place to live. Lobsters will not settle in open sandy areas, which are too soft to support burrows.

*Some types of lobsters like cold water, but this spiny lobster likes the tropical waters of the Caribbean.*

Wherever the living conditions are right, lobsters are sure to settle. These animals can be found just about everywhere in the tropics and subtropics, including the Mediterranean Sea and the Gulf of Mexico. Spiny lobsters are especially common in warm waters. Tropical areas are also the home of slipper lobsters, usually found on shallow, muddy bottoms.

Lobsters are plentiful in colder waters as well. Some cold-water spiny lobsters make their home in the chilly seas of southern Australia, New Zealand, and southern Africa. Likewise, the cool waters off the northeastern U.S. coast, England, Norway, Sweden, Germany, and France are packed with true lobsters. Smaller populations of these creatures can also be found in other areas around the world. The only places lobsters do not seem to live are in the frigid seas around the Arctic and Antarctic.

Most lobsters live in water no deeper than 150 feet. Some shallow-water species, however, travel to deeper water at certain times of the year. And deep-sea lobsters always stay in the dark depths of the sea. These small, pale creatures have been found miles below the ocean's surface.

## Segmented Bodies

All lobsters have segmented bodies. This means their bodies are made of a series of parts or segments attached one to the next, like the cars of a train. The segments are grouped into three main areas: the head (front section), the **thorax** (middle section), and the **abdomen**

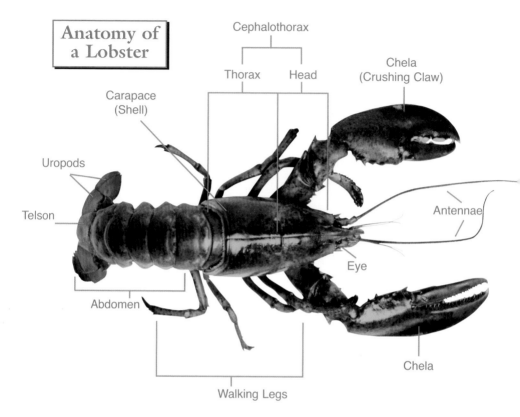

**Anatomy of a Lobster**

Cephalothorax

Thorax     Head

Chela (Crushing Claw)

Carapace (Shell)

Uropods

Telson

Antennae

Eye

Abdomen

Chela

Walking Legs

(rear section). The head and the thorax are connected to form a part called the **cephalothorax**. (*Cephalo* comes from a Greek word that means "head.")

The cephalothorax is the lobster's trunk. It contains all the important organs such as the brain, the stomach, and the heart. It also includes the lobster's mouth, eyes, and many sensory **appendages** (things that extend or stick out from the lobster's shell).

The abdomen, jutting out behind the cephalothorax, is sometimes called the tail. The abdomen is long and thick. It is divided into many visible segments. Each of these is covered by a hard plate. The plates are connected by flexible joints that let them move separately. These joints let the lobster bend its abdomen beneath its body whenever it likes.

The end of the lobster's abdomen looks like a fan. The middle section of the fan is called the **telson**. It is the last segment of the lobster's body. The outer sections of the tail fan are called **uropods**. Most lobsters have two uropods on each side of the telson.

## Many Limbs

Lobsters have many pairs of limbs. Five of these pairs are much larger than the others and are attached to the thorax segments. In many species, the first two thorax limbs end in powerful claws. Limbs that end in pinching claws are called **chelipeds**, and

*A lobster peeks out from under a ledge on the ocean bottom. Lobsters prefer to live in cracks or holes in rocks or coral reefs.*

the claws themselves are called **chelae** (singular chela). One chela is usually larger than the other, with blunt bumps on the inner edges. This is the crushing claw. The smaller chela is lined with sharp points for gripping and tearing.

After the first pair of limbs come the walking legs. These appendages are not as big as the first legs. The first two pairs of walking legs sometimes end in little claws that can grab small objects. The last two pairs usually end in simple points. These legs are used mostly for walking and sometimes for cleaning the abdomen.

Each segment of the abdomen also has a pair of limbs. These appendages are hidden beneath the lobster's body and cannot be seen from above. Most of the appendages are shaped like paddles and are called **swimmerets**. The swimmerets can beat to help the lobster move through the water. They also play an important role in reproduction.

In addition to their legs and swimmerets, lobsters have five pairs of limbs on the head. Two pairs act as **antennae** (sensory organs). Another pair is used for stuffing food into the mouth, and two pairs are used for chewing.

## A Hard Covering

The lobster's body is completely covered by a hard shell called an **exoskeleton**. The exoskeleton surrounds and protects the lobster's soft insides. It also supports the lobster's body because a lobster has no internal bones.

*A spiny lobster uses one pair of antennae to find food and the other to stuff the food into its mouth.*

If the exoskeleton were completely hard, of course, the lobster could not move, eat, or breathe. So in some places, such as the leg joints, the exoskeleton thins out. In these areas the exoskeleton is still sturdy enough to support the lobster, but it is thin enough to bend as needed. In other areas the exoskeleton contains holes that let food, water, and other materials pass into and out of the lobster's body.

The top and sides of the lobster's cephalothorax are covered by a part of the exoskeleton called the **carapace**. In most species the carapace is rounded. It usually ends in a pointed spine called the **rostrum**. The shape of the rostrum varies from species to species.

## Identifying Lobsters

The rostrum is not the only feature that changes from one lobster species to another. There are many other ways to tell these animals apart. Color, for instance, varies widely. Some lobsters are a greenish brown all over. Some are speckled with dots of yellow, brown,

*The body of this slipper lobster is flatter and thicker than the body of a spiny lobster or a true lobster.*

red, blue, black, and other shades. Some lobsters can even be red, blue, white, or other uniform colors all over their bodies.

The best way to tell lobsters apart, however, is by general body shape. True lobsters, with their large chelae, are easy to recognize. Spiny lobsters have huge antennae and no chelae. Slipper lobsters tend to be thick and flattened, with short chelipeds and walking legs. And deep-sea lobsters are usually small, with long, skinny chelipeds and delicate chelae.

But these differences are only skin-deep. No matter what they look like, lobsters of all species have a great deal in common. As a group, these animals create one of the most interesting families in the world's oceans.

# The Cycle of Life

L obsters can live a long time. Some species reach fifty years of age or even more if they do not get sick or caught by fishermen, or fall prey to other animals. Lobsters grow throughout their lives, so very old lobsters can be huge. The biggest lobster ever caught weighed more than forty-four pounds and measured three feet from tail tip to claw tip!

During its lifetime, a lobster follows a certain cycle. It hatches, changes, and builds a life and a home on the ocean floor. It gets bigger and stronger. Eventually it is able to mate and create a new generation of lobsters.

## Early Life

Lobsters start their lives as tiny creatures called **larvae**. The larvae do not look like adult lobsters. They are transparent, with big dark eye spots, and they are about one-sixth of an inch long.

A newly hatched larva floats to the ocean's surface. There, it enters the plankton, a rich soup of developing sea creatures. The lobster larva swims around in the plankton and eats any other tiny animals it can catch. Meanwhile, it tries to avoid being caught and eaten itself. If the larva is successful, it will grow. A lobster larva that stays alive long enough goes through three body changes over the course of several weeks. When the larva is done changing, it looks like a tiny lobster and measures about three-quarters of an inch from tip to tip. It is strong enough to swim up and down in the water.

*A lobster larva swims in the plankton on the surface of the ocean, looking for other tiny animals to eat.*

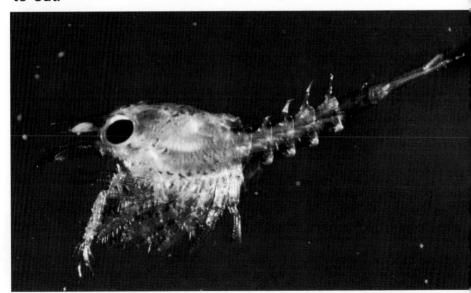

The little lobster is now ready to look for a home on the ocean floor. It makes its way downward, out of the plankton. If the lobster spots a good place to live, such as a shallow area with lots of small rocks, it settles to the bottom. If the area does not look good, the lobster swims upward again. It drifts a little longer on the ocean currents, then dives again to see if conditions have improved. The lobster does this again and again until it finds a suitable place to live. Then it settles to the sea floor and goes through another body change that prepares it for a bottom-dwelling lifestyle.

*A young lobster scurries around on the ocean floor looking for a permanent home.*

## Molting

New lobsters have a lot of growing to do before they reach adult size. Growth happens through a process called **molting**. When lobsters molt, they shed their old shell and create a new, bigger one.

To molt, a lobster first sucks in a great deal of water to make its soft inner body swell. The swelling puts pressure on the exoskeleton, and soon a crack appears on the upper shell between the carapace and the abdomen. The lobster lies on its side and starts to wiggle its inner body through the crack. The animal must work fast. Lobsters cannot breathe while they are molting, so they will suffocate if the process takes too long.

In most cases, molting is successful. Lobsters usually escape from their shells within a few minutes. Sometimes, however, the process takes more time. The trickiest part of a molt is pulling the thick flesh of the chelae through the narrow joints of the claws. A lobster can struggle with this task for quite a while. If nothing is working and a chela simply will not come loose, a lobster can detach the claw and leave it behind. It sacrifices the claw to save its life.

A newly molted lobster is soft and limp all over. Immediately it starts taking water into its flesh to inflate its body. When the lobster's shape returns to normal, the outer skin starts to harden. After a few days the lobster's new exoskeleton is rigid enough to provide some protection and support. It will be

*Since it found its permanent home on the ocean floor, this lobster is growing quickly and will molt several times during the next year.*

weeks or even months, however, before the new covering is completely hard.

Young lobsters molt often. During their first year on the ocean floor, these animals molt up to ten times. They molt less and less as they get older. By the time a lobster is between five and eight years old, it molts only once or twice a year. A lobster that has reached this stage is an adult, and it is ready to mate and produce larvae of its own.

## Mating

Mating usually happens during July, August, or September, when water temperatures are warmest. A female lobster initiates the mating process by finding a suitable male. She sends chemicals into the water to tell the male she wants to mate. In response, the male allows the female to enter his den. He watches the female carefully and touches her often. He is waiting for his mate to molt.

After a few days, the molting process takes place. The male starts a courtship dance as soon as the female escapes from her shell. He then flips the soft female onto her back and uses special appendages on his first tail segment to pass sperm into the female's body. This process takes a minute or less. When it is over, the female flips back over and crawls to a quiet corner of the male's den. She will stay there for a few days, until her new shell has hardened a little bit and she feels safe enough to leave.

After leaving the male's den, the female finds a new hiding place. She rests and waits for her exoskeleton to harden fully. This process may take a couple of months if the water is warm. In cold waters, however, it can take as long as a year.

## Lobster Eggs

When the exoskeleton is finally hard, the female is ready to lay her eggs. She rolls onto her back and curls her abdomen upward. She then starts to pass eggs along with a sticky slime out of an opening on one of her tail segments. The eggs are fertilized as they leave the body. The female beats her swimmerets to push the newly laid eggs to her lower abdomen, where they are cemented in place.

By the time the female is done, she has laid anywhere from ten thousand to one hundred thousand eggs. The final number depends on the female's size. Bigger lobsters lay more eggs. Each egg is about one millimeter across, and it is dark green or black. Together, the eggs look like clusters of tiny grapes or berries. For this reason fishermen say that lobsters with eggs are "in berry."

The female will carry her eggs for about a year. During this time she fans the eggs with her swimmerets to keep them clean. Slowly the eggs ripen and turn from their original dark color to a pale brown. This color change is a sign that the eggs are getting ready to hatch.

## A New Generation

The eggs hatch as they finish developing. The newly hatched larvae are still attached to the female's abdomen. Over time more and more eggs hatch, and more and more larvae cling to their mother.

After a short time the female is ready to release her newly hatched young. She lifts her abdomen and beats her swimmerets strongly to break the

*Thousands of eggs cling to the underside of a female lobster. She will carry the eggs for about a year.*

*Tiny transparent eggs change from dark to light as they near the time for hatching.*

"cement" holding the larvae in place. The little larvae immediately start to drift away from their mother. Before long they will reach the ocean surface. There, they will live in the plankton and start growing into adults.

Only a tiny fraction of the larvae will reach adulthood. Most will be eaten within the first few days of their lives. Many others will die from exposure after they cannot find a good place to settle. Scientists estimate, in fact, that only one out of every one thousand lobster larvae survives to adulthood. It is not a big number—but it is enough. As long as a few lobsters from each batch survive, ocean populations of these animals will continue to thrive.

# Staying Alive

L ike all animals, lobsters must eat to survive. These creatures are night hunters. They leave their dens after dark to search for snails, worms, crabs, clams, mussels, and other tasty treats. They will also eat fish if they can catch them. If a lobster cannot find living prey, it will snack on seaweed, algae, or even the remains of dead animals.

## Senses at Work

Before a lobster can eat a meal, it must find one. One way lobsters find prey is through their sense of smell. Smell sensors are found on the lobster's two small **antennules**, which grow from the head. A lobster continually flicks its antennules up and down to pick up chemicals floating in the water.

This information is then sent to the brain. There, it is translated into smell information that lets the lobster know the direction of its prey.

The sense of taste is also important to lobsters. Lobsters taste with thousands of tiny hairs that poke through the shells of their legs and mouthparts. Using these hairs, a lobster can taste something just by touching it. If the item seems like it might be good to eat, the lobster passes it to its mouth. The lobster then tastes the item one more time with its hairy mouthparts before deciding whether or not to gobble it down.

Sensory hairs also play an important role in the lobster's sense of touch. The carapace and antennae are sprinkled with tiny holes that let touch-sensitive hairs grow out into the water. Any time the hairs move, a lobster "reads" the movement to see what caused it. This sense is amazingly accurate. By using its hairs, the lobster can easily tell the difference between a direct touch, an ocean current, and the struggles of a dying fish.

## Limited Sight

The last sense lobsters use for hunting is sight. They have two stalked eyes on their heads. The eyes work in very dim light, so a lobster can use them even at night. But scientists think that lobsters see mostly movement and changes between darkness and light. They do not form clear pictures of objects or

*The light is dim on the ocean floor, but this lobster finds food by using its senses of touch and taste as well as sight.*

other animals, so sight probably is not as useful to the lobster as smell, taste, and touch.

## Eating a Meal

After a clawed lobster finds a meal, it grabs the food with its chelae. The lobster uses its large crushing claw to hold the prey and break its shell, if necessary. It uses its sharp-edged ripper claw to tear the prey's flesh into bite-size pieces. The lobster then transfers the chunks to its first walking legs. Small claws at the end of the legs seize the food and bring it to the lobster's mouth, where it is grabbed by a smaller set of limbs called the **maxillipeds**. These limbs hold the food in place while two more sets of limbs, the **maxillae**, further tear the food and pass it into the lobster's body.

*A hungry lobster uses its large claws to hold and tear apart its meal.*

Spiny lobsters do not have claws, so their eating method is slightly different. These lobsters look for sea urchins, clams, mussels, snails, and other slow-moving prey. They grab the prey with their jaws, which are strong enough to crush bones and shells. The maxillipeds and maxillae then process the food.

Once inside the body, food passes into the lobster's stomach. The stomach is lined with hard teeth that grind the food into a soft paste. This paste moves into the lobster's gut, where it is digested. Particles that cannot be digested pass through the system and are dropped as waste pellets.

## Avoiding Predators

Lobsters are not just hunters. They are also hunted by larger animals, including codfish, sand sharks, octopuses, skates, and many other creatures. To avoid these **predators**, lobsters stay out of sight as much as possible. They do this mostly by hiding in their burrows during the daytime and coming out to feed only after dark. A resting lobster may poke its head out of its burrow during daylight hours. Even if the lobster is seen, however, it is not in much danger of being pulled from its home. A lobster can retreat deep into its burrow if a predator approaches. It can also jam its limbs into rocky cracks to lodge itself firmly in place.

**Camouflage**, or protective coloring, also helps lobsters avoid being seen. Most lobsters have shells that match their surroundings. Lobsters that live in

Protective coloring helps a lobster hide from predators (right), but sometimes larger animals such as this sea turtle see through the disguise and catch a lobster meal.

dark areas, for example, may be dark all over. Reef lobsters, which live in shallow, sunny waters, are usually covered with patterns of stripes, spots, and bars that look like sunlight dancing on the ocean floor.

# Fighting for Survival

Sometimes disguise fails and a lobster comes face-to-face with a predator. If this happens, the lobster has several ways to defend itself. Making a fast escape is the easiest option, and it is the one the lobster will likely choose. Lobsters can move very quickly by using powerful muscles to yank their abdomens downward. This fanning movement creates a strong push that blasts the lobster backward through the water. The lobster repeats the tail flip over and over until it reaches a safe hiding place.

If escape is not possible, the lobster will fight to defend itself. The powerful chelae are the clawed lobster's main weapons. A lobster that feels threatened stands high on its walking legs and spreads its tail fan. It raises its open claws and holds them in front of its body in a defensive posture. This position sends the message that the lobster will attack if the predator moves any closer. Any animal that ignores the message will get a painful pinch.

Although spiny lobsters have no claws, they also have ways to protect themselves. These animals use their long, thorny antennae as weapons. A spiny lobster can flick its antennae like whips, striking hard enough to tear a predator's flesh. After such an attack, the startled predator usually backs off long enough to let the lobster escape.

Despite their defenses, lobsters are sometimes caught by predators. In this desperate situation, a lobster can detach its limbs or claws to free itself. If the lobster is lucky, the predator will not realize what is happening, and it will cling to the detached part while the lobster makes its escape. Once safe,

*When a lobster feels threatened by a predator, it raises its claws and holds them in front of its body.*

*This lobster can quickly escape from an enemy by using its strong muscles to flee backward through the water.*

the lobster will start working to regrow its missing limb. It will take several molts to complete the growth process, and the new limb may not look exactly like the one the lobster lost. But this is not a problem for the lobster. Looks are not important in the underwater world, and an oddly shaped limb is a small price to pay for survival.

# 4

# On the Move

M any scientists are interested in the day-to-day lives of lobsters. To learn more about lobsters in the wild, scientists have developed special tracking tags that give off electronic signals. Using scuba equipment, scientists enter the ocean, find lobsters, and attach the tags. After the scientists return to the surface, they can use computers to pick up the signals sent by the tags and track the lobsters wherever they go.

These and other studies have shown that lobsters are always on the move. These busy animals often roam widely during the night, when they are most active. They shift from place to place as the seasons change, and they may even travel long distances. Knowing these habits helps scientists guess where and when lobsters are likely to appear.

# Night Wanderers

Lobsters stay close to home during daylight hours. When night falls, however, they leave the safety of their shelters and set out across the ocean floor in search of food. A lobster walks quickly and covers a lot of ground. In a single night, this animal may travel as far as a quarter mile before turning around and heading back toward its home.

These nightly travels prove that lobsters have incredible navigational abilities. A lobster can find its way home on the darkest night. Even if a lobster is walking on a sandy bottom with no landmarks, it has no trouble retracing its path. Recent studies

*Lobsters are most active at night. In just one night, this spiny lobster can travel a half mile in search of food.*

suggest that lobsters have a kind of built-in compass that lets them read the earth's electrical fields just as a person might read a map. By using this extra sense, a lobster always knows exactly where it is. In one study, scientists removed spiny lobsters from their shelters and dropped them more than twenty miles away. When released, the lobsters did not act confused. They turned in the correct direction and immediately headed for home.

## Seasonal Migrations

Lobsters are also known to make seasonal **migrations**. Many lobster species prefer warm water. In the spring, abundant sunshine heats up the shallow waters close to shore. This temperature change attracts hordes of lobsters from deeper, colder waters. The lobsters stay in the shallow waters throughout the spring, summer, and early fall. As winter approaches, however, the lobsters leave their summer homes and head back out to sea. They do this because deep water is more stable and does not cool down as much as shallow water does during the winter months.

When studying lobster migration, scientists divide lobster populations into two types: "onshore" and "offshore." Onshore lobsters are those that live very close to land during the warm months. These animals typically travel five or six miles between their summer and winter homes. Offshore lobsters are those that live farther out at sea. These animals travel much farther than their onshore relatives. Some tagged offshore lobsters have walked hundreds of miles before settling down for the season.

## The Lobster March

The spiny lobsters of the Bahamas have a unique way of migrating. During the summer months, these creatures live in the shallow waters of the Great and Little Bahamas Banks. They keep to themselves, seldom mingling with other lobsters except to mate. Then, sometime in late October or early November, winter storms start moving in. The storms stir the once crystal clear waters of the Bahamas into a sandy soup. In response, the lobsters

*Spiny lobsters march in a line along the sandy bottom of the shallow waters in the Bahamas.*

begin to gather. They are preparing for the fifty-mile trek to their deepwater winter home.

Because this journey takes the lobsters across open, sandy bottoms, it is a dangerous trip. The lobsters have nowhere to hide if a shark or another predator attacks. To keep themselves as safe as possible, the lobsters travel in groups. One lobster leads the way. Another lobster uses its first pair of legs to grab the lead lobster's tail fan. A third lobster joins the lineup, then a fourth, and so on. Before long a column of up to sixty-five lobsters has formed. The lobsters march steadily forward, covering one-eighth to one-quarter mile per hour. They will not let go of each other for any reason, and they will not slow or stop until they reach their destination.

Although the "lobster march" is most common in the Bahamas, it can be seen in a few other places as well. The spiny lobsters of Belize, Bimini, Florida, and other hurricane-prone areas may also undertake mass migrations. Sometimes so many lobsters set off at once that their bodies blanket the ocean floor. Seen from above, shallow coastal waters appear red because of all the lobsters gathered below.

## Floating Larvae

Not all lobster movement is intentional. Some of the longest lobster "migrations" are made by larvae, which drift wherever ocean currents and winds take them. Scientists believe that some lobster larvae drift hundreds of miles before settling to the ocean floor.

Others may get caught in local currents and end up living very close to their hatching grounds.

Many studies have been done to learn more about larval movement. From these studies, scientists have discovered that lobsters in Maine's Penobscot Bay

*This tiny larva may end up hundreds of miles away from where it hatched by drifting on ocean currents.*

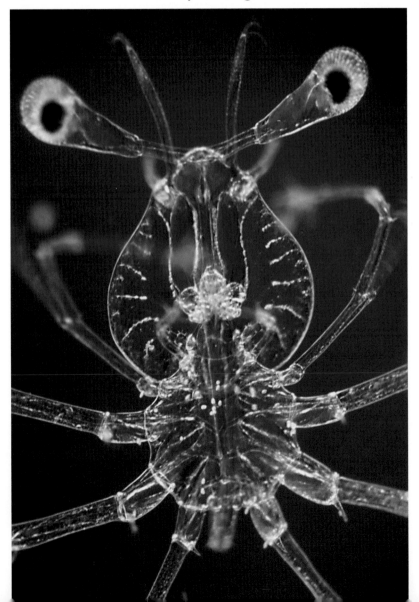

wash in from the ocean. Some of Florida's spiny lobsters hatch locally, get caught in circular currents, and settle close to home. Others catch a ride on the Florida Current from spawning areas in the Gulf of Mexico and the Caribbean. The rock lobsters of Queensland, Australia, hatch in breeding grounds off the Queensland coast and in the Gulf of Papua. The larvae spend four to six months drifting in a circular current between Australia and Papua New Guinea and travel up to 1,250 miles before finally dropping to the ocean floor.

## Lobster Populations

Understanding larval movement is an important part of understanding lobster populations in general. Because young lobsters may not settle near their hatching grounds, there is no guarantee that a lobster-rich area will stay that way. Even small changes in ocean conditions from year to year can have big effects on how lobsters spread out in the ocean. This in turn can create problems for lobster fishermen, who depend on these animals for their living. Luckily for fishermen, ocean currents and winds are fairly stable over time. This means that lobster populations are also fairly stable. Unless the world's climate changes dramatically, these amazing animals will continue to settle in the same areas they have roamed for millions of years.

# Glossary

**abdomen:** The last section of the lobster's body, also called the tail.

**antennae:** Motion-sensing organs on a lobster's head.

**antennules:** Taste-sensing organs on a lobster's head.

**appendages:** Limbs or other body parts attached to a lobster's segments.

**camouflage:** Coloring that helps a lobster blend into the background.

**carapace:** The hard shell that covers a lobster's cephalothorax.

**cephalothorax:** The lobster's joined head and thorax.

**chelae:** A lobster's claws.

**chelipeds:** Lobster limbs that end in pinching claws.

**crustaceans:** Hard-shelled animals with segmented bodies and antennae.

**exoskeleton:** A hard outer skeleton that surrounds and protects a lobster's body.

**larvae:** The name for newly hatched lobsters until they change into their adult form.

maxillae: Mouth limbs that tear food into small pieces.

maxillipeds: Mouth limbs that hold food while it is eaten.

migrations: Seasonal relocations, usually from colder waters to warmer ones.

molting: Shedding the exoskeleton.

predators: Animals that hunt other animals to survive.

rostrum: A spike at the front of a lobster's carapace.

swimmerets: Paddle-shaped appendages beneath a lobster's tail.

telson: The middle part of the lobster's tail fan.

thorax: The middle section of the lobster's body.

uropods: The outer parts of the lobster's tail fan.

# For Further Exploration

## Books

Mary M. Cerullo, *Lobsters: Gangsters of the Sea*. New York: Cobblehill, 1994. This book takes an in-depth look at the Maine lobster. It includes a lot of information on the New England lobster industry.

Ethan Howland, *The Lobster War*. Chicago: Cricket, 2001. This fiction book tells the story of Dain, a teenager who tries to make a living lobstering.

Allison Lassieur, *Crabs, Lobsters, and Shrimps*. New York: Franklin Watts, 2003. This book explores the relationship between lobsters and their closest relatives, crabs and shrimps.

## Periodical

William F. Herrnkind, "Strange March of the Spiny Lobster," *National Geographic*, June 1975. This article focuses on the migrating spiny lobsters of the Bahamas.

## Web Sites

**Enchanted Learning Lobster** (www.enchanted learning.com/subjects/invertebrates/crustacean/

Lobsterprintout.shtml). This site includes basic lobster information and a good anatomy drawing to print out and color.

**Gulf of Maine Aquarium, Lobsters** (http://octopus. gma.org/lobsters). This site includes information about the lobster life cycle, boats, tales and trivia, and more. It even includes some fun lobster activities.

# Index

# picture credits

# about the author

Kris Hirschmann has written more than one hundred books for children. She is the president of The Word-shop, a business that provides a variety of writing and editorial services. She holds a bachelor's degree in psychology from Dartmouth College in Hanover, New Hampshire. Hirschmann lives just outside Orlando, Florida, with her husband, Michael, and her daughters, Nikki and Erika.